Original title:
Through the Windows of the Soul

Copyright © 2025 Creative Arts Management OÜ
All rights reserved.

Author: Elias Marchant
ISBN HARDBACK: 978-1-80587-046-3
ISBN PAPERBACK: 978-1-80587-516-1

Fragments of a Soul's Canvas

In a jigsaw of dreams, pieces misplace,
A cat saw a mouse, ran with grace.
Colors of laughter spill on the floor,
My inner spark needs a little more.

The Veil of Inner Silence

Whispers of giggles and thoughts on the shelf,
The mirror grins back, not my true self.
Bubbles of wisdom float in some stew,
Each droplet a secret, just me and my shoe.

Hues of Emotions Untold

Paint splatters bloom in a garish delight,
My heart wears polka dots, oh what a sight!
When feelings erupt like a well-mixed drink,
I slip on a banana peel, then laugh till I sink.

Secrets in the Gaze

Eyes like a circus, juggling dreams bright,
Caught in a stare that feels just right.
With a wink and a nudge, we dance around,
In this gazing game, absurdity's found.

Spirals of Silent Awareness

I peek inside, I see a dance,
A swirling jest within a glance.
The thoughts all twirl in silly ways,
In laughter's grip, the mind astrays.

Colors splash like paint from a can,
With pastel dreams, both bold and bland.
A tumble of giggles fills the air,
As whimsy plays without a care.

Whispers of quirks in every hue,
Tickle the senses, anew and true.
Conversations in an unseen thread,
Wink and nod, but words, they fled.

Amid these spirals, I chuckle still,
At thoughts that dance with such a thrill.
A secret world behind my eyes,
Where humor hides, a sweet surprise.

Tapestry of the Unseen Journey

We weave our tales with threads of jest,
In patterns strange, they seem the best.
Each twist reveals a twisty plot,
In stitches tight, we find the spot.

Oh, look! A cat in a polka dot,
A flying fish, a dancing tot.
These visions swirl, a quirky blend,
Where rules of sense begin to bend.

Unveiled at last, the truth is bright,
A tapestry of pure delight.
In every corner, laughter hides,
Where sheer absurdity abides.

The journey winds with silly flair,
Each step we take, a giggle rare.
In threads unseen, our stories sing,
A tapestry of joy we bring.

The Heart's Unwritten Script

My heart writes tales with funny flair,
A comedy show beyond compare.
It scribbles joy on every page,
Each laugh a dance, a wild stage.

The plot twists like a puppy's play,
Each chapter ends with bright hoorays.
Oh, what a tale of mishaps grand,
Written with love by my own hand.

Luminescence of the Invisible

I see giggles in the air we breathe,
Dancing shadows, what a reprieve!
Like light bulbs that wink in the night,
They spark the mundane with pure delight.

Invisible friends, they join the fun,
Making mischief till the day is done.
They tickle my thoughts, poke my mind,
With jokes that only groaners can find.

Portals to My Essence

My essence giggles, a silly surprise,
A mirror of laughter seen in my eyes.
Each look's a portal, a window wide,
Where humor bursts forth like a joyful tide.

The faces I make could crack a stone,
Like cartoons brought to life, well-known.
In children's plays, I sometimes partake,
Making the world laugh, oh, for goodness' sake!

The Unfolding of Inner Landscapes

In landscapes bright where giggles bloom,
My inner world dispels the gloom.
Each tree's a joke, each hill a grin,
Where laughter begins and never thins.

The rivers chuckle, the clouds just tease,
Winds whisper secrets that aim to please.
With every step, a punchline spry,
Unfolding joy as I wander by.

Introspection's Pathway

In the mirror, I see my face,
Is that really me, or a funny place?
A happy ghost, with a silly grin,
Chasing thoughts like they're made of tin.

Hiccups of laughter escape every thought,
As I ponder the wisdom my pet has sought.
Each moment's a joke, or so they say,
Oh, the antics that dance in my mind's play!

Beyond the Gaze of Existence

Peering deep into my brain's own nook,
I found a rabbit, reading a book!
He chuckled, 'Life's a circus and I'm the clown,
Try juggling dreams; don't let them drown!'

With thoughts that wiggle and bounce around,
Every idea is a lost and found.
I chased one, but it laughed and flew,
'Try a little harder, I'm just messing with you!'

Mirrors of the Conscious Mind

Reflective thoughts in a wobbly glass,
What's deeper? A secret, or just sass?
My brain does the tango, teaches me to sway,
With every reflection, it's a new ballet.

Wit and whimsy flip-flop in line,
Dancing thoughts, oh what a design!
I trip on the puns that lay in wait,
Like a clown shoe'd grin; it's never too late!

Soft Silhouettes of Emotion

Shadows whisper on the wall,
Each one teases with a playful call.
One's a jester; the other a king,
Together they chuckle at everything.

In a world of giggles and playful sighs,
My heart takes flight, as the little lies
Tell stories of joy wrapped in mirth,
With each soft silhouette, I bounce on earth!

The Tapestry of Whispers

In a world where giggles reign,
Every glance reveals a grain.
A wink, a nudge, unspoken glee,
A silent joke between you and me.

Do you see that cat in the hat?
It's plotting schemes, imagine that!
With feline stealth, it prowls the floor,
Sneaking snacks from the kitchen door.

The sprinkle of laughter, the chuckles shared,
Moments unfiltered, a friendship declared.
Like chocolate ice cream on a summer day,
Sweet surprises come out to play.

With every glance, we find a tale,
Of merry pranks that never pale.
In this patchwork of giggles and gasps,
Life's humor plays, and joy unclasped.

Fathoms of Untamed Journeys

Adventures await in every look,
Like pirate maps in an old storybook.
A treasure chest filled with grins,
As we sail on waves of whimsical spins.

Each glance a compass, directing fun,
Guiding us to where the laughter's begun.
With silly hats and mismatched socks,
We dance with joy, revealing our blocks.

There's a giggle in the depth of the sea,
Mermaids and dolphins all laugh with glee.
Let's dive below, where antics are grand,
And ride the bubbles, hand in hand.

In corners where sunlight barely creeps,
Secrets emerge in the quiet, it peeps.
With every journey, so wild and true,
We laugh at ourselves—how about you?

Soliloquies of the Heart

Whispers of joy spill from the soul,
Heartbeats drum a merry stroll.
A dance of quirks, a fleeting glance,
Life's a stage, come join the dance.

Mix-ups and mishaps paint the scene,
A twirl here, a near miss, oh what a routine!
With each misstep, the laughter grows,
As flailing arms make perfect prose.

Unraveled thoughts as we giggle aloud,
Stripped of silence, we sing proud.
The heart's soliloquy, a comical play,
With every beat, it finds a way.

So let your joys spill like spilled ink,
In a whimsical world, where hearts wink.
In moments of humor, we truly bloom,
Dancing together, we conquer the room.

Curtains of Perception Lifted

Curtains rise, the show begins,
Our playful laughter always wins.
With quirks on display, let's embrace,
The comedy written on every face.

A misfit's charm, it shines so bright,
Chasing shadows in the morning light.
With lemonade giggles and peanut fights,
We craft our stories, full of delights.

The lens of life, a funny view,
Finding humor in the mundane too.
Like grandmothers knitting with yarn so thin,
Patching up dreams where the fun begins.

So peek through the gaps of daily grind,
In the silly moments, greatness you'll find.
With each curtain lifted, joy reigns supreme,
Life's a comedy, a whimsical dream.

The Echoing Chambers of the Heart

A pigeon coos, it's not my phone,
Is that a text or just alone?
It flutters by, with stolen crumbs,
Life's issues? A joke, it hums.

Inside my chest, the beats collide,
Like two left feet on a fun ride.
My heart's a drum, a silly beat,
Dancing to pizza, can't be beat!

With every thump, it does a jig,
A little crazy, not that big.
The laughter echoes, a joyful sound,
In chambers where love can be found.

So here's the truth, as it unfolds,
My heart's a jester, breaking molds.
Amidst the chaos, joy is found,
In laughter's grip, we're truly bound.

Murmurs in the Depth of Stillness

A whisper floats like a balloon,
In quiet rooms, it laughs at noon.
The cat just sighed, a solemn breath,
In stillness so loud, it defies death.

The fridge hums tunes from days of yore,
While socks conspire on the clean floor.
The silence speaks, it's quite the trick,
A fleeting thought that plays a kick.

In still waters, odd things float,
A rubber duck in a far-off moat.
It quacks at life, a fierce debate,
As murmurs rise, we celebrate.

A cozy chair creaks like old bones,
Each groan's a tale of ancient tones.
Amidst the calm, we find our fun,
With silly thoughts, our minds do run.

The Light that Bends Within

A wink of light, it plays the fool,
It twists and turns, a merry duel.
Each beam that's bent begins to dance,
In shadows, bright, it takes a chance.

Reflections smile on every wall,
It teases me, I can't help but sprawl.
The lamp just grinned, a cheeky spark,
In corners dark, it leaves its mark.

With every turn, it finds new ways,
To brighten up my gloomy days.
The light that bends, it knows the score,
In laughter, joy, it's never bore.

So follow light, with open eyes,
It winks and grins, it never lies.
In every shimmer, a jest is spun,
And in that glow, we share the fun.

Colorful Threads of the Unseen

A spider weaves in neon hues,
Her web's a tapestry of blues.
With threads of laughter, spun so tight,
She catches dreams in morning light.

Unseen colors, a vibrant show,
They tickle noses, making you go,
With every thread, a tale is spun,
Of whimsy's dance and endless fun.

In laughter's quilt, we find our way,
Each stitch a smile in disarray.
With fabric light as morning air,
We spin our stories, without a care.

So here's to threads, both bright and bold,
In every twist, a joy untold.
The unseen tapestry of our plight,
We wear with pride, a colorful light.

Radiance in the Quiet Corners

In the corners where shadows play,
A sock puppet gave a grand ballet.
The cat was judging from its throne,
While dust bunnies rolled like foam.

A teapot hummed a jazzy tune,
As spoons danced under the light of noon.
An old chair groaned, throwing a fit,
Saying, 'Why must I always sit?'

The cupboard chuckled at the joke,
As potted plants began to poke.
Each petal shared a silly thought,
In bright corners where laughter's caught.

Unseen Horizons of Desire

A squirrel dreams of a pizza slice,
While plotting schemes that aren't too nice.
His cousin mocks with a nutty grin,
'You think you'll taste that? Where'd you begin?'

The moonlight winks and says, 'Not yet!'
As fireflies toss in a grand duet.
They twirl and spin, their hopes alight,
Romancing dreams deep into the night.

A raccoon checks off his wish list,
But finds that garbage bins are just missed.
He sighs and thinks of cheesecakes rare,
While the night air whispers, 'Just beware!'

The Heart's Hidden Gallery

In a closet full of mismatched socks,
Lies a masterpiece that truly rocks.
It's a painting made of old receipts,
Of love and laughter, quite the feats.

A mirror reflects a million grins,
As old shoes ponder where they've been.
Each button has a story to share,
Of striped blunders and plaid despair.

The light flickers in a playful glow,
As photographs flaunt their laughable show.
There's a family made of mismatched parts,
Their beauty lies in unique hearts.

Worlds Behind a Façade

Behind the curtain, a cat throws shade,
As ants rehearse their grand parade.
The goldfish dreams of Broadway fame,
In a tank where it's not too tame.

A broomstick is a wizard's ride,
While a spider watches with keen pride.
Each lost shoe is a prince in disguise,
A kingdom lost between goodbyes.

A blender whispers sweet nothings,
While fries plot their crispy offerings.
Cups share secrets in hushed delight,
Of baking mishaps gone out of sight.

Where Thoughts Take Flight

A pigeon perched on a sill,
Staring back like a grumpy drill.
My thoughts take off on tiny wings,
Over rooftops, oh the joy it brings!

In the midst of a coffee spill,
I ponder life, with slight distill.
Are those clouds made of cotton candy?
I giggle—a flight of thoughts so dandy!

What if socks could start to talk,
In mismatched pairs, they'd take a walk?
With comments sharp as a tack,
Designs so wild, they'll never lack!

So here I sit, a chair my throne,
With wacky musings all my own.
The world can be a whacky play,
Where thoughts take flight and laugh all day!

Dreams Caught in a Web

A spider spins with flair and grace,
While dreams dance on, in a silly race.
Caught among webs of cotton thread,
Each thought is woven, happily fed.

In the corner, a sock seems to glow,
With secrets of lands we do not know.
It giggles at dreams all snug and neat,
In this web, the light and stars do meet.

Oh, how my mind can twist and twine!
Like spaghetti and meatballs, so divine!
I wonder if bees drink their tea,
In tiny cups, just like you and me?

With each thought stuck in her glue,
The spider spins a world brand new.
So catch your dreams, let laughter flow,
In this web, it's a marvelous show!

Windows of the Mind's Eye

Opened brightly, a curious gaze,
Peeking out in a whimsical haze.
What's it like beyond this frame?
A parade of clowns? Oh, what a game!

With jellybeans falling from the sky,
I spot a giraffe wearing a tie.
A trampoline bounces on fluffy clouds,
While unicorns prance; they're so loud!

I laugh as I spot my favorite chair,
Dancing around, floating in the air.
Pigeons in tuxedos shuffling near,
Making a ruckus, oh dear, oh dear!

This window's view, a joyful spree,
Where nonsense reigns, wild and free.
So come on, join this frisky ride,
In the madness where dreams abide!

The Depths of Silent Reverie

In a quiet corner, thoughts do dangle,
Like socks on a line, quite the wrangle.
They whisper secrets, quips, and glee,
In the depths of a mind, so carefree!

I ponder absurdities with a grin,
Like why do cats always look so thin?
With fish in bowties tossing around,
It's a circus of thoughts, oh what a sound!

I drift with a giggle, lost in delight,
Where pop-corns dance and stars take flight.
With every tick-tock of a silly clock,
Time juggles moments, it's quite the mock!

So let us dive deep, without a care,
Into this reverie, rich and rare.
Where laughter echoes, thoughts intertwine,
In the depths of silence, we brightly shine!

Traces of the Heart's Journey

A heart wears glasses, quite the sight,
With smudged reflections, day and night.
It giggles at love's absurd call,
While tripping on dreams, it dances and falls.

A cookie jar's lid holds secrets dear,
It whispers sweet nothings, lending an ear.
With crumbs of laughter strewn about,
It finds joy in the chaos, without a doubt.

A map drawn in ketchup, twisting and turns,
Adventures unfurl as the world churns.
In the circus of feelings, it juggles with glee,
Each emotion a clown, wild and free!

So toast to the journey, with a wink and a grin,
For every wild twist, there's a giggle within.
In the heart's little journey, we laugh and we roam,
With pizzazz in the chaos, we find our true home.

Where Spirit Meets Silence

In the library of thoughts, dust bunnies play,
Whispers of laughter drift softly away.
A book falls open, it tells a good joke,
With wits so sharp, it could cut through smoke.

The quiet hum of a light bulb's flick,
Flickering ideas that dance and kick.
It groans like an old chair, making its plea,
Join us for tea, won't you teeter with me?

Mirrors reflect whispers of bubbles and cheer,
With every crack, new stories appear.
The spirit of silence wears shoes that squeak,
As echoes of giggles are all we can seek.

So here we sit, in a soft little nook,
Pouring our hearts into a whimsical book.
Where silence and spirit are partners in crime,
Creating a rhythm, a dance in their time.

Illuminated by Intrinsic Truths

A lightbulb flickers, it can't settle down,
Radiating thoughts that wear a fun crown.
Truth laughs aloud, wearing mismatched socks,
Playing hide and seek among colorful clocks.

The mirror giggles, it's seeing double,
Reflecting the chaos and moments of trouble.
It dances in shadows, a peek-a-boo friend,
Unraveling knots that can twist and bend.

An owl in a bow tie hoots at the night,
Sharing secrets with stars in a whimsical flight.
On the dance floor of wisdom, wisdom wears shoes,
Tap dancing through life, with nothing to lose.

So let's toast the truths, with a giggle and cheer,
For laughter and insight are always quite near.
In the glow of our hearts, with silliness broad,
We find our way through the cosmic facade.

The Quiet Resonance Within

A teacup trembles with secrets galore,
Spilling hot tales on the kitchen floor.
Each drop a giggle, a splash of delight,
Laughter echoes softly through day and night.

A feather floats down from the sky so wide,
Bringing whispers of joy, like a whimsied slide.
It tickles our thoughts, makes us snort and beam,
In this sea of silence, we frolic and dream.

Grumpy old socks in a laundry race,
Trust in the toss, they'll find their place.
Amongst the spinning, there's joy in the grime,
With suds of laughter, we dance through time.

So let's hum a tune, from the core of our soul,
With humor as compass, it makes us whole.
In this quiet resonance, laughter's the key,
Unlocking the joy, that's forever free!

Reflections of a Hidden Landscape

In the mirror, a squirrel grins wide,
Chasing its tail, it tries to hide.
An acorn in hand, a feast on the ground,
It thinks the whole forest is its playground.

The trees nod along with a chuckling breeze,
While ants march by like small armies at ease.
A raccoon in shades plans his next big heist,
Laughing at shadows, oh what a feast!

Clouds roll in, a parade of great fluff,
But even the sun knows when things get tough.
Who knew the sky could be such a joker?
As light plays tricks, getting much bolder.

A pond reflects all the nonsense around,
A frog in a bowtie just leaped with a sound.
It croaks a tune that makes no sense,
While nature laughs, it's pure hilarity hence.

The Journey into Self-Luminescence

A light bulb flickers in the dark of my brain,
It thinks it's a star, what a hilarious gain!
With thoughts that may glow, like neon so bright,
I wander in circles, oh what a delight!

Reflection reveals my odd little quirks,
Like dancing with shadows that wiggle and jerk.
A laugh from the mirror says, "What a show!"
With giggles and snorts, I steal the glow.

Each ponder leads to pathways unknown,
Among all the puns, my humor has grown.
Illuminating fears with a pun or two,
Brightening up, like a sparkly dew.

So here I am, in the haze of a jest,
Finding the light in my own silly quest.
With every bright thought that tickles my mind,
I stay luminous, oh what a find!

Windows to the Uncharted Depth

Peering in, a pizza pie awaits,
Greeting the world through cheesy plates.
The toppings a map of uncharted scenes,
Where mushrooms dance and pepperoni dreams.

I dive into flavors, a bold expedition,
Sailing through slices, what a mission!
Each bite a wave of guffaws and surprise,
With laughter and crumbs, oh such a prize.

Ahoy, brave fork, I declare it a feast!
An adventure of taste, to say the least.
And as the last crust begins to retreat,
I'm left with giggles, feeling quite neat.

With empty plates and a heart full of cheer,
I raise a toast to my colleagues near.
For in this dining, where joy does erupt,
I find my own depths, all doughy and plump!

Lighthouses in Voids of Solitude

In solitude's corner, a beacon does laugh,
Shining its light like a goofy gaff.
It calls to the lost, saying, "Come take a look!"
While seagulls plot chaos from their own little nook.

A lighthouse stands tall with its stripes of bright hues,
Telling tales of the ships it has helped to choose.
With each ever-swaying beam of its glow,
It winks at the fog, putting on quite a show.

The rocks below giggle at tides that ace,
As waves crash in rhythm, they dance with grace.
Amongst solitude, laughter paves way,
Brightening the emptiness of each gray day.

So here in this calm, where silence can reign,
I find humor in lighthouses, keeping me sane.
For even in stillness, where shadows may drool,
There's joy in the journey, as light's just a fool!

Glimmers of Inner Light

My neighbor's cat walked by, oh wow,
Wearing sunglasses — who taught her how?
A grin on my face, I can't help but laugh,
As she struts like a queen on her regal path.

In the depths of my mind, I see silly sights,
Like penguins in tuxedos having dinner fights.
A toast with a fish — what a crazy spread!
If only my thoughts could be so well-bred.

Inside every heart, a jester resides,
Making jokes while the serious side hides.
I tip my hat to the quirks that we share,
For laughter's the light that we all can declare.

So let's dance with our dreams, let them twirl and spin,
A ballet of whims where the fun can begin.
Wave goodbye to the frowns, let the chuckles unfold,
In the glimmers of light, may our antics be bold!

Reflections in Quiet Waters

A duck in a bow tie just paddled by,
Thinking he's fancy, oh my, oh my!
With a quack and a flip, he poses for cheers,
While I choke on laughter and snort through my tears.

The pond seems to giggle beneath the warm sun,
As frogs have a meeting—oh, the ribbiting fun!
They're bouncing ideas on lily pads bright,
Debating if flies prefer left or right.

I tossed in a pebble, it rippled the scene,
A splash of surprise, like a movie routine.
Why do I imagine they plot all day long?
In the whispers of water, they sing me their song.

So here I remain, with a grin on my face,
In the company of ducks, at my own happy place.
To dive into laughter, a curious fate,
Where reflections of joy eagerly await.

Shadows Beneath the Surface

Beneath my bed, there's a monster, they say,
But I think it's just my socks on display.
With mismatched patterns and a wink in their stride,
They plot their great escape, with nowhere to hide.

Old shadows dance like they've lost their way,
Two left feet stumbling, come join the ballet!
With a whoosh and a twirl, they're out of the light,
Who knew that old dust could put up a fight?

In the closet, a hat with a feather quite bold,
Claims it's the king of the stories retold.
Juggling dreams like a circus in flight,
I giggle and wonder what else hides from sight.

So here's to the shadows that bring us a grin,
Making mischief while we settle in.
For laughter shall reign, wherever we roam,
In the corners and crevices that we call home!

Echoes of the Heart's Whisper

In a world of whispers, I heard a slight "beep,"
Was it the toaster, or dreams in a heap?
They chirp like the birds that forgot how to sing,
Each chirp a reminder of joy they can bring.

The heart did a jig, while my stomach did flip,
As thoughts lined up nicely for a jokester's trip.
Why did the chicken cross, do you recall?
To chuck a few puns at the party ball!

A ladybug danced on the rim of my cup,
Inviting a laugh, oh, I had to erupt!
With wings like confetti, she fluttered about,
Turns out all my worries were lost in her sprout.

So let's raise a toast to the echoes we find,
In laughter and joy, oh so sweetly entwined.
From whispers to roars, let our spirits rejoice,
In the symphony of life, let's all raise our voice!

Starlight in the Depths of Eyes

In the twinkle of a wink, I spy,
A universe of giggles, oh my!
When you blink twice, a star takes flight,
Cosmic jokes dancing in the night.

Cartwheeling thoughts in every stare,
Seeing pizza slices up in the air!
A comet trips on a beam of light,
While planets chuckle at the fright.

Eyes that sparkle, stories untold,
Fables of laughter, daring and bold.
In every glance, a balloon goes pop,
Joyful chaos that never can stop.

So let's gaze and giggle, gaze and grin,
In this sparkling realm where we both swim!
With every blink, our worlds collide,
There's starlight in your giggles, it can't hide.

Veils Lifting in Inner Realms

Peeking past the curtain, what do I see?
A parade of clowns on a mind's marquee.
Silly hats and a neon blue nose,
In the land of thoughts where laughter flows.

With every veil that flings aside,
A fresh punchline appears, and we both ride.
Jokes hiding just behind a smile,
Let's unravel them, it's worth the while!

Oh, the silliness that we're unveiling,
Like a puppy who's caught its tail, flailing!
Every layer gone, brings a joke or two,
In inner realms, there's so much to do!

So let's peel the layers, just have some fun,
In the carnival of thoughts, we've just begun.
With each veil lifted, laughter ensues,
In this circus of minds, we'll never lose.

The Symphony of Hidden Whispers

In a concert hall of thoughts, we sit,
Whispers of wit that just won't quit.
A serenade of giggles takes flight,
As melodies twist and turn through the night.

An orchestra of chuckles, sounds so bright,
With each laugh, the world feels just right.
Tickles and snickers form a sweet tune,
As we dance under a giggling moon.

Like a playful breeze through the trees,
Hidden whispers float on the easy breeze.
Every note carries a silly surprise,
Laughter bursting like confetti in the skies!

So let the symphony play on and on,
With each hidden note, our cares are gone.
In this joyful rapture, let's sway and spin,
For the music of laughter is where we begin.

Navigating the Labyrinth of Emotions

Welcome to the maze, oh what a ride!
With walls made of giggles, let's not hide.
Around every corner, a punchline peeks,
In this goofy labyrinth, joy leaks!

Twists and turns create comedic surprise,
Finding joy, like candy, for our eyes.
Every tear of laughter, a path we trace,
As we run in circles, caught in the chase.

So hold my hand, let's wander these lanes,
The tickles of laughter release our chains.
Where emotions bounce like rubber balls,
Making merry echoes in these hallowed halls!

With each step forward, we stumble and play,
Turning frowns to giggles in a magical way.
In this labyrinth of joy, we'll forever roam,
For laughter, dear friend, is our true home.

Chasing Shadows of the Spirit

I saw a ghost with a silly grin,
Waving at me, trying to win.
Danced in circles, so full of cheer,
Said, "Why are you staring? Come join me here!"

I stumbled and tripped on my own two feet,
As it slid away, light and fleet.
"Hey, come back! We could have some fun!"
It laughed and vanished, oh what a run!

I pondered aloud, is it friend or foe?
With every encounter, more seeds to sow.
Chasing shadows, with spirits divine,
So many giggles, a great punchline!

In the end, were they real or mere jest?
Do shadows play games, or is it all a test?
I chuckled alone, as I walked away,
Who knew a ghost could brighten my day?

Whispers from the Inner Abyss

In the deep of my mind, things start to stir,
Whispered tales of my cat and her fur.
"Feed me more tuna!" I hear her shout,
An abyss of treats, now that's a route!

Underneath layers of wisdom and fun,
Lies a purring spirit, seeking a bun.
"What's the meaning of life?" I ponder anew,
She blinks and replies, "More naps, it's true!"

The abyss isn't dark, it's a curl-up space,
Where every thought comes with a whiskered face.
And every decision brings laughter to play,
Until cat decides that it's time for a sway!

With whispers so soft, I hear them cheer,
For inner musings, I hold so dear.
Filled with giggles and curls of delight,
My abyss in shadows, oh what a sight!

The Silences That Speak

In the silent room, the clock ticks loud,
Whispers of thoughts, dancing in a crowd.
A sock on the floor gives a knowing glance,
"Time to clean up! Don't you want to dance?"

The chairs all giggle, do they feel the weight?
Of all my mishaps, they watch and wait.
A dust bunny leaps, in a daring bound,
In silence it shouts, "Look what I found!"

The walls hold secrets, murmurs and sighs,
Every creak and groan, like comical lies.
A silent chuckle, a playful tease,
In this room of echoes, all senses at ease.

Yet every stillness has so much to share,
As laughter sneaks in, light as the air.
With silences deep and thoughts that collide,
I welcome their whispers, in mirth they reside!

Depths of Elysian Echoes

In the depths of my dreams, echoes do bounce,
Past silly adventures, each one I pronounce.
A unicorn sneezes, confetti in flight,
Turning the night into sparkles of light!

Down in Elysium, I'm king of the jest,
With fish that wear hats, oh what a fest!
They swim through the air with style so grand,
While I crack jokes like I'm in a band.

Every echo that rings, a sarcastic sound,
Tickling moments, as joy spins around.
I laugh with a dragon, who juggles three pies,
In this whimsical world, where fun never dies.

So here in the depths of absurdity's bliss,
I cherish the echoes, and all that I miss.
With laughter as treasure, oh what a spree,
In realms of the silly, there's room for me!

Whispers Beneath the Surface

In the depths, a ticklish sound,
A giggle lurking all around.
Fish inside the joke take flight,
A splash of laughter, pure delight.

Bubbles rise with silly tales,
Of dancing crabs and floppy snails.
Secrets swimming, never gory,
What a funny, fishy story!

Wink from frogs, a playful tease,
A chorus joins, as if to please.
Charming echoes mesh with cheer,
Life's a punchline, crystal clear.

So dive deep, but don't be shy,
For humor swims where dreams comply.
Let every splash become your song,
And find that giggle all along.

Shadows of the Unseen Heart

In corners dark, a quirky plot,
Where shadows dance, a funny thought.
A pair of socks lost in the fray,
Join in on jokes beneath the gray.

A heart that tickles, beats away,
With laughter hiding in its sway.
Why did the heart need a rest?
It got too tired at its jest!

Whispers float on shadows' breeze,
Of playful banter with such ease.
Echoing chuckles, light and silly,
As if the dark were really frilly.

So stroll through life with mishaps bright,
Where shadows blend with sheer delight.
Dance with whimsy, be absurd,
For laughter speaks without a word.

Echoes in the Depths of Being

In the abyss, echoes play,
A paper boat just drifted away.
With giggles bopping on a whim,
Life's a carnival, let's not swim!

A treasure chest of puns and jest,
Hides in corners, a cheeky fest.
Beneath the waves, the fish all chuckle,
As octopuses do the shuffle!

Echoes ripple in playful tones,
Jokes bounce off the ocean's moans.
Why did the crab never share?
Because it was a little shellfish, fair!

So dive in deep, let laughter roam,
Bubbles rise, you're far from home.
In every splash, let joy take flight,
For echoes linger, pure delight.

Lenses of the Silent Mind

Peeking through a quirky lens,
The world's a riot, full of pence!
Silly faces in the glass,
Where even penguins take a pass.

Balanced thoughts on tightropes sway,
With funny hats for every play.
Why did the mind wear shades all day?
To block out thoughts that went astray!

A silent giggle, loud and clear,
The lenses laugh when we're near.
They wink and nod at all we see,
Imagination's wild spree.

So calibrate your thoughts to smile,
In this wonderland, take a while.
Let laughter guide what's hard to find,
Through lenses bright, the silly mind.

The Ethereal Window Within

In a room that's filled with sunlight,
A cat thinks it's a lion, oh what a sight!
Chasing shadows, dodging dust bunnies,
Living life with endless, silly honeys.

A flower pot becomes a throne,
Where thoughts wander far from home.
The radio plays a tune so bright,
While socks dance in the morning light.

Imagining a world that's upside down,
Where fish wear hats and dogs wear crowns.
Every giggle echoes in the air,
In a carnival of thoughts laid bare.

Oh, the silliness of every glance,
As dreams take flight in a fanciful dance.
Life is but a playful jest,
In this quirky heart, I find my rest.

Luminescent Pathways of the Mind

Balloons float high with cheeky glee,
As gnomes plot mischief by the old oak tree.
Thoughts bounce around like playful deer,
In a mind that finds joy in silly cheer.

Rainbows sprout from every idea,
While daydreams glide on cola, oh dear!
The toaster talks back, gasps in surprise,
As toast leaps out to wave goodbye.

Laughter weaves through each crack and seam,
Creating a fabric of a delightful dream.
Comics dance and biographies spin,
As the mind warms up for a joyful win.

Juggling the thoughts that feel just right,
Cactus in a top hat steals the night.
With every chuckle, joy finds its way,
In this playful realm, I long to stay.

Mosaics of Silent Melodies

Silent whispers echo like a song,
As mismatched socks in a drawer belong.
Each tune is a whisper, soft and sweet,
Painting laughter with every beat.

A noodle dances on the kitchen floor,
While wooden spoons dream of living more.
As spaghetti twirls, oh what a sight,
In the grand banquet of quirky delight.

Painted pies giggle and tease,
While cupcakes plot a sugar-laced breeze.
Chocolate fountains bubble with glee,
In this mosaic of joy's jubilee.

Ripples of laughter fill the air,
As giggles and snacks create a fair.
With musings sweet, the night grows old,
In these silent melodies, stories unfold.

Echoes of Forgotten Dreams

In a closet of long-lost schemes,
Curly wigs play hide and seek with dreams.
While old tricycles rust and sigh,
The echo of laughter dances high.

Mismatched buttons jive and sway,
Humming tunes that come out to play.
Each silly note forms a bright charade,
As forgotten dreams waltz in a cascade.

Odd socks chatter, secrets unfold,
Sharing gags in rags of bold.
The echoes bounce like bubbles in air,
Tickling hearts with joy to spare.

In this carnival of the past,
Each chuckle blooms and wishes cast.
So let your dreams ride this silly beam,
For laughter's the treasure in every theme.

Colors of the Unspoken

There's a pink squeaky toy in my heart,
It hops, it dances, it plays every part.
My laughter's a rainbow, oh so bright,
In a world made of giggles, pure delight.

Each sigh is a color, a splash on the wall,
Like rainbows in puddles after a fall.
I wear polka dots under my serious clothes,
While my secret dance party starts and then glows.

Sunshine on Tuesday, I trip with a grin,
Painting my thoughts that swirl and spin.
My soul's a canvas, wild and grand,
With crayons and giggles, I take a stand.

In this art gallery of chuckles and fun,
Who needs the moon when I shine like the sun?
So grab a paintbrush, let's make it a spree,
Colors of nonsense, just wait and see!

Light and Shadow Intertwined

There's a shadow named Fred who loves to tease,
He hides in the corners and sneezes with ease.
He pokes at my light, plays peek-a-boo,
Giggling softly, just me and my crew.

Sunshine tickles the edges of gloom,
As jokes dance around like a bright-colored bloom.
Banana peels lurking by old dusty chairs,
Tell me who put that there, oh how life dares!

I trip over laughter, I stumble on cheer,
The shadows all whisper, but I never fear.
As light wraps around me, I twirl in delight,
A silly parade on this oddball night.

So let's shake our shadows, give them a show,
With playful banter and tickles, let's go!
In this circus of darkness, we'll shout, what a blend,
For laughter's the light that will never end!

Glimmers of Inner Light

In a world made of giggles, a sparkle appears,
It twirls with a grin, calming all fears.
Each giggle a beacon that shines up ahead,
Bouncing through laughter, like bouncing on bread.

Marshmallows whisper secrets at night,
As stars play charades, a hilarious sight.
The moon wears pajamas and dances with flair,
While I munch on stardust without a care.

Glimmers of nonsense are found in the air,
Jokes flutter by as we dance in a pair.
Each chuckle a twinkle, a wink from above,
In the comedy stage of this life that I love.

So let's leap like bunnies from dawn until dusk,
With the joy that we carry, the laughter we thrust.
For glimmers are funny, and that's what I seek,
In a world of hilarity, it's joy that we speak!

Reflections in Forgotten Glass

In the dusty old mirror, my laugh skips along,
With a poodle named Pickles who hums a sweet song.
We wink at our echoes, both silly and bright,
Conducting a symphony deep in the night.

Dust bunnies dance in a two-step rapture,
While I juggle my thoughts with a quirky new chapter.
The reflections are giggles, all missed but not lost,
Like socks in the dryer, we'll never count the cost!

So here's to the glasses, both cracked and pristine,
Where laughter's the polish, a whimsical sheen.
In rooms full of echoes, we shimmer and play,
Celebrating oddities, come join the bouquet!

Beyond these four walls, let the nonsense flow,
With each friendly laugh, our spirits will grow.
So let's toast to reflections, both funny and crass,
In this carnival of life, let the moments amass!

Emotions Flowing like Rivers

My tears would swim and splash about,
As if they dreamed of a fun-filled route.
Joy jumps like fish in a comedic stream,
While worries paddle, caught in a meme.

Laughter floats like a leaf on top,
A giggle cascade that never might stop.
With grins that ripple and shouts that pour,
Emotions flow, a whimsical lore.

Ducks quack jokes, and frogs sing tunes,
In this water park where joy communes.
A tidal wave of bliss, so absurd,
Life's punchlines come when they're least heard.

So grab your boat, let's sail together,
In this river of feelings, shine like a feather.
We'll ride the waves, we'll splash, and we'll sway,
Emotions flowing, come join the fray!

The Paintbrush of Inner Vision

With brushes tucked in pockets deep,
I color dreams as I awake from sleep.
A tangerine smile, a cerulean frown,
I paint the world's quirks in a vibrant crown.

Each stroke is laughter, a canvas of fun,
My palette's a party that won't be outdone.
Doodles of chaos and swirls of glee,
I slap on colors like confetti spree.

A dash of purple for a silly dance,
I twirl the hues like a comic romance.
Swatches of chaos, a masterpiece lacks,
I'll paint the world vibrant, so don't hold back!

So grab a brush, let's scribble in style,
With strokes that tickle and brush that beguile.
We'll make a mess, oh what a sight!
In this hilariously crafted delight!

Layers of Unseen Realities

Beneath my skin lies a clown parade,
Where giggles hide and silliness played.
My layers peel off, each one a joke,
A comedy show for the senses to stoke.

First, a giggle like a tickling breeze,
Then a chortle that aims to please.
A burst of laughter, a silly surprise,
As I sift through the layers, the humor flies.

Each layer revealed is a dance of wit,
Jokes ricochet, but never they quit.
Beneath the chaos, a sweet punchline waits,
Layered laughter that always elates.

So let's strip it down, uncover the fun,
Life's multiple layers, one by one.
In the depths of my soul, a jesting spree,
Layered realities, come join me free!

Radiance in the Inward Glance

A peek inside shows a circus quite bright,
Where worries juggle and joy takes flight.
Clowns wearing smiles and tigers who yawn,
A glowing self with quirkiness drawn.

With inner beams of radiant cheer,
I glow like a lamp, spreading joy far and near.
Confetti of thoughts like fireflies pop,
In this radiant world, let laughter drop.

As I glance within, hilarity spills,
The giggles ignite like wind on hills.
In this playful nook, a world unfurls,
Where silliness reigns and laughter twirls.

So come take a gander, a light-hearted chance,
To twirl through my thoughts in a joyful dance.
With radiance glowing, the fun will enhance,
Join the merry circus of inward trance!

The Intimacy of Unexpressed Thoughts

In silent halls where secrets dwell,
The mind's a jester, casting spells.
Thoughts dance like squirrels in a tree,
Chasing their tails, wild and free.

Giggles trapped in a mind's embrace,
Witty remarks hide from their place.
Peeking out from behind shy walls,
Like clowns waiting for laughter's calls.

The heart grins wide, but lips stay tight,
Trading quiet secrets for a bite.
A joke's on you if you can't hear,
The chuckle bubbling just so near.

In this play of silence, we conspire,
A world of humor, dreams, and fire.
Whimsical whispers, oh what a show,
In the heart's theater, laughter will flow.

Dreamscapes of Inner Whimsy

In dreams, a monkey wears a gown,
He jumps around, trying not to frown.
The clouds are made of cotton candy,
While unicorns dance, quite dandy.

Tickling stars with a feathered hand,
They giggle as they take a stand.
A river flows with chocolate cheer,
Wishing for visits throughout the year.

With mismatched socks and shoes so bright,
The moon plays tag with the night.
As pillows float on breezy wings,
Our thoughts become the silliest things.

In these whimsies, let's take a leap,
Where laughter's a treasure, oh so deep.
With each new dream, we take a ride,
In the carnival where giggles abide.

The Soul's Silent Dialogues

In whispers soft, the thoughts take flight,
A chat with the soul, hidden in light.
Like cats with yarn, they tangle and twist,
Sassy retorts that can't be missed.

Beneath the surface, a playful jest,
The heart of the matter, a worn-out vest.
Pokes at the spirit, nudges the will,
Like a tickle fight that gives a thrill.

What if pineapples wore big hats?
Would they sing or just mingle with bats?
In this silence, laughter's the key,
Unlocking the giggles that set us free.

An orchestra playing without a sound,
With shadows and giggles spinning around.
Say more with silence, let hearts discern,
Where humor and thought flicker and burn.

Murmurs Beneath Fractured Facades

Behind the mask, a circus plays,
With juggling thoughts in a comical craze.
A mime mimics all that we hide,
Turning our worries to fun we confide.

Cackles and whispers blend and collide,
As thoughts tap dance, they can't run and hide.
Chess pieces though wooden, giggle in jest,
In a world where laughter takes the best.

Fractured facades, yet humor stays bright,
What lies beneath brings pure delight.
Each grin's a puzzle, each laugh's a clue,
On this canvas of chaos, we'll bloom anew.

So let the murmurs reach your ears,
For the cracks in the silence hold light and cheers.
In the language of laughter, find what's whole,
Even fractured facades can cradle the soul.

Serendipities in the Dark

In the night, a sock takes flight,
Landing on my cat's delight.
Laughter echoes, shadows play,
As he pounces, slips away.

A spoon dances, spoils the plan,
Chasing crumbs, a tiny fan.
Cackles rise as we all trip,
In our midnight snack attack grip!

Unexpected giggles flow,
When the fridge gives a loud hello.
Out of nowhere, tunes do start,
With each mishap, we just cart!

So in the dark where quirks collide,
Small joys bloom, no need to hide.
Serendipity's wild embrace,
In the fun, we've found our place.

Threads of Connection Unseen

A tangled mess of yarn and thread,
Knots of laughter, joy widespread.
Grandma stitches, what a scene,
Each mishap makes her plans obscene!

A call from dad, his voice all snug,
Confused my name with that of a bug.
We burst with laughter, can't hold tight,
At the silly mix-up in our sight.

Birds exchange gossip on the line,
While dogs conspire to steal our dine.
Hovering clouds laugh, they just might,
Pencil us in for a playful flight!

So through these threads, unseen yet clear,
Connections bloom, bring us near.
With joy and jest, we intertwine,
In this fabric, we're just fine.

The Heart's Cryptic Navigation

Maps are drawn with crayon hues,
Leading hearts to hidden views.
A treasure hunt where clues are sly,
With giggles shared and winks that fly.

Detours taken, paths so strange,
Find a donut shop in range.
Every wrong turn leads to cheer,
Finding joy, our goal is clear!

With friends we roam, a motley crew,
Sharing secrets, silly too.
Laughter echoes in the air,
Navigating hearts with flair.

Cryptic signals, smiles unfold,
In this journey, we are bold.
Each twist and turn brings light and glee,
As we wander, wild and free.

Beyond the Surface of Sight

Behind the curtain, jokes reside,
A surprise party, friends collide.
They can't see me, I'm in disguise,
Peeking through, with playful eyes.

Balloons float, giggles abound,
With cake crumbs scattered all around.
In the chaos, joy does spark,
Shining bright, it's our hallmark.

Secret glances, oh what fun,
Mystery games can weigh a ton.
Finding treasures in the mess,
Laughter's the key to the excess.

So even when the light grows dim,
Chasing giggles, we won't swim.
Beyond what meets the eye, we play,
In this humor, we find our way.

Soulful Vibrations in Silence

In a quiet room, my thoughts do dance,
A sock on my foot? A life circumstance!
Whispers of giggles float through the air,
Echoes of humor, for those who dare.

I ponder the wisdom of my pet cat,
Is he a philosopher or just a brat?
His judgment is swift as he paws at the floor,
A furry sage, who sleeps and snores.

I look in the mirror, a reflection grins,
With toothpaste on lips, and a dab of chins.
Did I really think that I could look cool?
Instead, it's a laugh, not a dignity rule.

So I humor the world with my silly plight,
And dance in the silence, a joyous sight.
Each moment is quirky, with joy on the rise,
Beneath the calm surface, a world full of spies.

Elysium of Internal Reflections

In my mind's garden, the daffodils sway,
I trip on a thought, then I tumble and play.
Reflection's a game with a twist and a flip,
A belly laugh here, and a chuckle there, sip!

Clouds in my head form strange shapes and styles,
A cloud shaped like toast makes me laugh for a while.
Why not have breakfast while pondering life,
With crumbs of humor and a sprinkle of strife?

With each little giggle, I find something bright,
A pondering angle that brings pure delight.
Life's a riddle wrapped up in a jest,
A cosmic punchline that keeps us impressed.

So dance in the daydreams, embrace silly schemes,
In the labyrinth of mind, we find our true beams.
The inner world chuckles, a chorus of cheer,
In the Elysium where laughter is near.

The Mirage of Self-Discovery

I stroll through my thoughts, a whimsical haze,
Where socks lose their pairs in a comical phase.
Each step is a giggle, each twist is absurd,
A parade of ideas, in silence unheard.

The mirror reflects a curious face,
With spaghetti for hair, in outrageous space.
I wink at the silly, my dreams have a flair,
In this mirage, I find laughter to spare.

Maybe I'm wise, or just a huge clown,
In the circus of wisdom, I wear a frown.
Yet each cringe-worthy thought brings a smile,
As I tumble and tumble all the while.

Self-discovery's more like a fun ride,
With cotton candy clouds and funny things tried.
So I'll embrace the mirage, the twists of my mind,
In this playful journey, true joy I shall find.

Tidal Waves of Serene Awareness

In the ocean of thought, I surf and I glide,
On waves made of wonders, where silliness hides.
A splash of a giggle, a wave of delight,
Dancing with shadows, lost in the light.

I ride the tide where reflections bask,
What's my next question, I wear like a mask?
A jellyfish thought, floats gracefully by,
With a grin on its face, as it waves goodbye.

Awareness flows in like a grand tidal show,
As I ponder the secrets of fish below.
They swim with such purpose, with no need to care,
While I'm here just swimming, in laughter to share.

Oh, the waves of awareness, how they tease and they play,

With ripples of joy, that brighten the gray.
So let's dive and discover this ocean so fine,
For the humor of life provides the best sign.

The Ethereal Orbs of Feeling

In the chamber of my chest, a bouncing ball,
It rolls with joy and makes me sprawl.
With laughter echoing, it gives a tease,
Oh, the orbs of feeling, they aim to please.

When sadness drops like a soggy biscuit,
I chase it round, what a strange visit!
It winks at me—like a Cheshire cat,
Those orbs are tricky, imagine that!

Happiness dances in a jolly parade,
Oddly shaped floats that never fade.
I juggle my giggles, they slip and slide,
As I bounce through life, what a wild ride!

So here's to those orbs, so wild and free,
That tickle my heart with their curious glee.
In the funhouse of feelings, I'm lost in the fray,
With a grin on my face, I laugh all the way.

Celestial Maps of Introspection

On a cloudy night, I search the stars,
With maps in my mind, I'm off to Mars.
The constellations wink, creating a fuss,
Drawing giggles from a cosmic bus.

I traced my dreams on a pizza slice,
Mushrooms and pepperoni; oh, isn't that nice?
As the universe chuckles, I ponder my fate,
Is this pizza delivery or a celestial date?

Those maps twist and turn like a corkscrew's dance,
Leading me where I least expect to prance.
With a telescope lens, I spy on my aim,
Finding joy in the oddest game!

So I wander through skies of opinion and thought,
Collecting weird notions, all freshly caught.
As I sketch my own route with marker and flair,
I laugh at the mysteries that linger in air.

Frosted Windows of Reflection

On frosted panes, my breath creates art,
A snowman with glasses, oh—where to start?
I giggle at snowflakes that melt in the sun,
A race with the warmth, oh, isn't it fun?

Reflecting my thoughts, they shimmer and move,
A dance of confusion with each little groove.
The ice sings a tune, a chill in the space,
As I tug on my mittens, I'll keep up the pace.

With every swipe, I reshape my own face,
A silly grin forms; I win this race!
The world huffs and puffs, blowing out steam,
As I draw little suns—what a wacky dream!

So here's to the frosty, oh-so-crafty scene,
With giggles and grins that keep life so keen.
In the art of reflections, I find my own roll,
With laughter that sparkles, brightening my soul.

Kaleidoscopes of Inner Narratives

In my mind's kaleidoscope, colors collide,
Twisting and turning, what a silly ride!
With glitter and marbles, my thoughts take flight,
Creating a spectacle, pure delight.

Each turn reveals stories, some odd, some bright,
Dancing on whimsy, in daydreams of light.
A parade of chimeras, they strut with finesse,
While I sip my tea, I must confess!

Oh, the patterns of giggles churn and swirl,
As I spin through the tales, my thoughts start to twirl.
Like jellybeans tumbling in a wondrous spree,
I chuckle at life—it's just too funny!

So let's toast with candy, to narratives bold,
With laughter in layers, a joy to behold.
In this kaleidoscope, I take my sweet stand,
With a wink and a chuckle, life's just grand!

Chasing Secrets of the Self

In the mirror, my hair's a spree,
A wild dance of hair gel glee.
Yet behind this chaotic guise,
Are dreams hidden, oh, what a prize!

I wear these socks, one blue, one green,
As if fashion's a game, not serene.
My heart's a jester, playing tricks,
Hiding truths among the flicks.

I laugh at my thoughts like they're a stand,
Juggling secrets with a shaky hand.
Beneath the giggles, I stack my fears,
Like a clown, dodging all my tears.

But in this circus of the brain,
I find the joy in every pain.
For life's a joke, so don't take heed,
Unraveling giggles is the only need!

Tides of Unspoken Thoughts

My brain's a beach, waves crash and swell,
With whispers of thoughts, trapped in a shell.
They sneak away like sand in my toes,
Unspoken words nobody knows.

I built a castle with hopes and fears,
Then watched it crumble, still dry my tears.
Seagulls caw at the depths of my mind,
Searching for treasures, none that they find.

Each tide pulls back, revealing more,
Of laughter, blunders, and thoughts galore.
Yet sillyness hides in the depths of night,
Like a starfish hiding till dawn's first light.

So in this ocean of giggling ghosts,
I'll ride the waves and raise a toast!
To all the thoughts I'll let run free,
Let them dance like sand on the spree!

Gazing into the Abyss of Feelings

Peering down a well so deep,
Where my thoughts bubble and laugh, not weep.
What lurks inside? A cheeky clown,
Throwing pies where my worries drown.

The deeper I look, the more I see,
A pool of giggles rushing at me.
Feelings tangled, oh, what a mess,
Like socks after a game of chess.

With every glance, a new surprise,
A rubber chicken in disguise!
So I dive in with giddy grace,
Splashes of humor, oh what a place!

Though shadows loom and toss the light,
I chase the chuckles, it feels so right.
In this abyss of whimsy and play,
I find a joy that's here to stay!

The Ethereal Dance of Vulnerability

In the ballroom of my quaking heart,
I twirl and stumble, oh, a fine art!
With every dip, a giggle escapes,
A waltz of worries in funny shapes.

With floppy shoes and mismatched ties,
I lead with laughter, oh, how it flies!
Each step I take reveals a giggle,
And spins my fears into a wiggle.

The spotlight shines on my playful mask,
In this dance, I need not to ask.
For every toe I step upon,
Brings a chuckle, where once was a yawn.

So let's embrace this jolly mélange,
In our foxtrot of flaws, let's take the chance.
For in this dance of brave delight,
We twirl in humor, banishing fright!

The View from Within

I peek out today, what do I see?
A squirrel in a tie, sipping his tea.
The sun wears a hat, so jaunty and bright,
While clouds play hide-and-seek, what a sight!

A cat on a skateboard rolls past my door,
Chasing its tail like it's wanting more.
The postman is dancing, delivering mail,
Caught up in a whirl, it's a lively tale!

The garden's alive with chatter and song,
Two flowers debating who's right or wrong.
The trees shake their leaves, let's all have a ball,
As laughter erupts, it's a festive call!

So I sit by my glass, with a grin that won't fade,
Life's quirks are a treasure, not one to evade.
Each glance that I take, fills my soul with glee,
What a wonderful world, come join me for tea!

Each Pane a Secret

Looking out my glass, a world goes by,
The neighbor's pet llama gives dancing a try.
It's wearing a tutu, so pink and so bright,
Jumping with gusto from morning till night.

The mailboxes gossip with stories to share,
One's got a postcard from snowy despair.
While the roses are laughing at weeds in a frock,
All of this unfolding, oh what a shock!

A bee in a bowtie buzzes past with flair,
Finding a flower to twirl with great care.
The sky wears a grin, up there it reveals,
Life can be silly, with hilarious feels!

I spot the old cat, he's judging the show,
With a monocle perched, oh how he can glow!
So much to discover with each little glance,
Life's windows are open, come join in the dance!

Veils of the Heart's Canvas

I swing back the curtain, what do I find?
Birds in a band, they're practicing blind.
A pig in a bowler, is learning to swim,
While fish in a tuxedo breathe rhythms on whim.

The goldfish are gossiping, sharing the scoop,
And one has a dream to join in the troop.
The flowers're all painting a mural so grand,
With colors exploding, a magical band!

A frog with a top hat croaks out a tune,
Claiming the right to the flower's full bloom.
While fairies are giggling, and chasing their tails,
Creating a breeze with their whimsical gales!

So I lean out, chuckling at this lively play,
With every odd glimpse brightening my day.
Laughter's a canvas, let colors unfurl,
In the grandest of galleries, let joy whirl!

Gazing Beyond the Veil

Peeking past the drapes, a sight none can beat,
A chicken on roller skates, isn't that sweet?
With a wig made of feathers, it zips with delight,
As it races the breeze, what a comical sight!

The clouds are all juggling, it's quite a display,
While rain drops are tap dancing along the way.
A squirrel adjudicator calls out the score,
"Ten out of ten, you can always do more!"

The garden gnomes gossip, as sunlight doth dance,
Plotting their scheming and giving a glance.
In every small moment, joy bursts at the seam,
It's laughter that flows, like a whimsical dream!

With each quirky scene that unfolds at a glance,
Life too is a stage, come join in the dance.
Round and round, let our spirits unroll,
The wonders of whimsy are good for the soul!

www.ingramcontent.com/pod-product-compliance
Lightning Source LLC
Chambersburg PA
CBHW060135230426
43661CB00003B/429